25 October 1415

The Battle of Agincourt, Henry V's Longbowmen Defeat The French

A Historical Narrative by

DecisiveDays

www.decisivedays.com

25 October 1415: The Battle of Agincourt, Henry V's Longbowmen Defeat The French

First Edition

November, 2013

ISBN-10: 0-9887705-6-3
ISBN-13: 978-0-9887705-6-0

v.0706

Please Note

The following is a highly detailed and graphic account of the events of 25 October 1415. If you are easily shocked, offended, or disturbed by descriptions of violent events, please return this title immediately for a refund.

This is an original text written and edited by several trained historians and history enthusiasts. As with all historical events, some details are in dispute; we chose to present what we thought most likely happened, in narrative format, in Parts 1-7 of this book. Plus there is a bonus chapter at the end about the English Longbow, a weapon that was very important to the outcome of this battle.

An online companion guide has been assembled that includes additional resources, as well as a free draft copy of our next book to be released, available here:
DecisiveDays.com/agincourt

Thank you,
David J. Kosmider
Founder, DecisiveDays

DecisiveDays

We produce short narratives on important days in history.

10% of all author royalties are donated to awesome non-profit organizations.

Details available on our website.

www.DecisiveDays.com

Questions or comments?

Email us:
news@decisivedays.com

25 October 1415

Contents

Prologue

The Battle of Agincourt was a part of a larger series of conflicts known as the Hundred Years War. At that point in history, Henry V was on the English throne, and the mentally ill Charles VI was the king of France. When Henry became king in April 1413, he was determined to press his claim for the French throne. The English kings had disputed the French line of succession since Edward III had claimed to be the only true heir to his uncle, King Charles IV of France, who died without a male child.

Even as he sent repeated delegations to the French to negotiate, Henry prepared for war. During the winter of 1414-15 Henry's officers began to commandeer ships for the transportation of the English army. The following August, Henry took his army across the channel to Harfleur and held siege to the town. By the 22 September 1415, when it appeared that the French army was not coming to help, the leaders of Harfleur finally surrendered.

The siege had taken much longer than expected and cost many lives. It was too late in the campaign season for much more action and most of his advisers urged Henry to head home, but the young king believed God was on his side and wanted to achieve something more than the capture of a single town. He settled on a plan to march the remainder of his army 100 miles from Harfleur to the English fortress at Calais. If the English army could walk unopposed through the countryside, this would be a major embarrassment for the French.

The march was slowed by blocked river crossings, but after finding a way to the other side, and marching through the town of Frévent, just 30 miles from Calais, they were caught, on 24 October 1415 near a small castle named Azincourt, by the full might of the French army. They were guarding the road to Calais.

The leaders of the two sides met, and in the elaborately formal custom of medieval chivalry, decided there would be a battle the next day, the feast day of Saints Crispin and Crispinian.

As the two armies settled down for the night, the French celebrated, drinking wine and playing games, expecting an easy victory and plenty of rich prisoners the next day. Henry meanwhile ordered his men to remain absolutely silent to guard against a surprise attack. No attack came in the night though and the following narrative tells the story of what was to become known as the Battle of Agincourt.

Part 1:
Waiting for Battle

The archers grew restless as the hours crawled by, and the king realised that he must attack, or stand and starve.
-Robert Hardy

25 October 1415. The sun rises and the men of the English army rise with it, though they had slept little after finding out the night before that they would finally fight. This is a sorry, bedraggled force. Of the ten thousand men who had set sail from England, only five thousand archers and less than a thousand men-at-arms still stood able to fight. They are shivering from the morning cold and are soaked through from the rain that did not

let up all through the night. Rust is slowly stiffening the joints of those with armor, and their blades are losing their edge.

They are famished; having set out with only eight days worth of provisions for what has become a difficult three week march across the French countryside. Getting by on what little they could forage, they are now close to the point of starvation. Many are still sick with dysentery as well, the same illness which had killed many of their comrades during the siege of Harfleur. Their stomachs are rumbling, their bowels beyond control, and their muscles are aching from the march.

Across half a mile of farmland, on a defensible plateau, the French stand watching the English as their countless banners wave in the wind, many still drunk from celebrating the night before. Vastly superior in numbers, well fed and rested, their armor gleaming in the sunlight, the very sight of them force the English to wonder if they will ever make it home.

Between the two armies is a swathe of open field, its soil freshly ploughed and soaked to a thick mud. The road to Calais and safety runs straight down the middle that field, through the center of the French lines. It is the English army's only hope, and it is a desolate one. The one crumb of comfort they can take as they assess the scene is that there are woods covering both sides of the English line, which would make it difficult for the French to outflank them.

Henry, fifth of his name to rule England, and claimant to the throne of France, is putting his army in order. Archers are gathering on the flanks while his small force of armored fighting men are in the center. The remaining men-at-arms, knights and those rich enough for armor and horses, are the military elite, but now they find themselves relying on common archers, many of whom they had fought against in recent Welsh wars. They feel safe in the knowledge that these peasants will obey and defend their superiors, but in truth they have more in common with the enemy than with these archers.

Henry is twenty-seven years old, tall and muscular, dressed from head to toe in gleaming plate armor. He does nothing to hide the scar on his face from the Welsh arrow that struck him while on campaign just over ten years ago. He rides down the lines, telling his men what he firmly believes, and what they needed to hear—right was on their side; God was with them; they would triumph no matter the odds. All of his soldiers are on foot, and at the center of the line he descends to join them. In his brown eyes glow the fire of absolute faith.

This is a man who had burned heretics before he ascended the throne, who had taken three masses before taking the field, who had even hung one of his own soldiers a few days previously for stealing from a French church. He does not just believe God was on his side, he knows it, and that certainty helps to quell some of his mens' fear. He has been King for just over two years and has spent that entire time trying to take back the French throne, that he believed was rightly his, first by negotiation, and now by war.

Following Henry's lead, the whole English army kneels, kissing the ground at their feet, and take a morsel of dirt in their mouths. Six thousand men share a common communion, a fighting man's Eucharist. Many still wear the bedraggled red crosses of St. George that they had sewn on at Harfleur, matching the banner under which they marched. That banner flies at the center of the army, along with the King's colors and those of the Trinity and St. Edward the Confessor. This is all the pomp that the English need.

The French, in contrast, are a riot of color. Most of them are men-at-arms, with heraldic silk tabards over their armor. Above them fly the flags of hundreds of nobles, men normally busy tearing France apart with their feuding. And among the banners is the huge, red silk Oriflamme, the sign that that no prisoners would be taken this day. Of course, this was just for show, the only thought on the mind of most of these French soldiers was how many rich English prisoners they could take for themselves by nightfall.

Though many of the common English bowmen might not know it, they face an army as divided by national interest as the English are united. Frenchmen of the rival Burgundian and Armagnac factions are eyeing each other warily as they wait. And wait they did.

Part 2:
Rain of Arrows

The first sound was the bowstrings, the snap of five
thousand hemp cords being tightened by stressed yew, and
that sound was like the devil's harpstrings being plucked.
-Bernard Cornwell

Both sides know that in battle, the army that advances first loses some of its advantage. The French hold back their desire for glory, waiting on their enemies' desperation. The small English force, half-starved and isolated in a foreign land, desperately need to reach Calais and safe passage home.

Hours pass, both sides staring across the field

at the men they would soon kill.

It is Henry who finally breaks the deadlock. Knowing that he must act, he decides that victory lay not with the nobles around him, but with the bowmen on their flanks. He orders grey-haired veteran Sir Thomas Erpingham to advance the archers.

Nervously, the archers advance from the protection of the stakes they had hammered into the mud. Clad, at best, in scraps of armor, many of them naked from the waist down after casting aside breaches ruined by dysentery, the archers are the most vulnerable men on the field. Knowing that every moment they delay is another moment they stand exposed to a French charge, they yank their stakes from the ground and hurry forward. Stopping just within bowshot of the French, they hammer the stakes back in with hefty mallets, forming a hedge of forward pointing spikes.

With the archers in place, the English men-at-arms advance to join them; eyes fixed on the French throng before them. Disorganization prevents French cavalry or archers from making the most of the bowmens' advance, but this luck could not hold.

Shoulder to shoulder with old friends from back home, men who had served together through this short but wearying campaign, the English form up again in the face of the French.

At last, Erpingham tosses his commander's baton into the air. It twirls beneath grey skies. This is the signal for the archers to release their arrows. The battle has begun.

The sky is dark with arrows, thousands of them falling in a vicious cloud towards the French lines, hissing like a deadly swarm. At this range the English cannot make use of their deadly armor-piercing bodkin arrowheads, but a lucky broadhead can still pierce a gap in the armor and snatch away a man's life. Even when it does no permanent damage, the force carried by the projectile is sometimes enough to knock a man off balance. The French lower their visors and raise their shields as they wait for the first round of arrows to hit.

Part 3:
The First Wave

The ground was sodden with the autumn rain and planted with young wheat, producing a slippery and glutinous mess underfoot that must have been especially tiring for the men in armour.
-Matthew Bennett

The flower of French chivalry will not stand idle while they were bombarded by peasants. Pressed by the English bowmen, it is their turn to advance. Cavalry burst forth from the French wings, galloping towards the archers, the ground rumbling at the sound of their charge.

The English bowmen stand steady, lowering

their aim to shoot straight into the chaotic mass of horsemen. Armored men gallop towards them at terrifying speed, but the archers hold their ground and keep firing. Men and horses fall into the mud. Injured horses turn tail and flee, out of their riders' control. Those few horses who reach the English lines veer away from the chest-high stakes, throwing their riders into the mud and galloping back the way they had come or dieing where they fall. The charge is broken.

There is to be no respite for the English. Forming into a column to make themselves less of a target, the French front line approach. A gleaming mass of faceless bodies in plate metal, this force alone outnumbers the whole English army.

The French stomp forward across the field, its broken ground churned to a muddy mess by the failed cavalry charge. Each step is a struggle as they try to retain their balance, isolated from each other within the confines of their armor, unable to see beyond the mud and the men around them.

The English rain arrows down from the flanks, as many as sixty thousand a minute fall upon the French column. Most bounce off their armor, creating a fearsome, rattling din, but some find their mark and dead men fall into the mud to be trampled. Instinctively, the French troops draw themselves together, becoming packed into a tight mass, jamming elbow to elbow in a clanking mob.

For all the damage the archers have done, things still look bad for the English. The French column hits like a battering ram, pushing the thin line of English men-at-arms back a dozen feet. Men fight to keep their footing, to hold their ground in the face of the attack, to stay steady as their formation wavers.

A brutal melee begins, men hacking at each other with swords, maces, and poleaxes. Their armor rings to the sound of blows, muscles straining to swing with all their might. There is grunting and screaming and the thud of colliding bodies.

The experience is a wretched one for the French. Worn out from their half mile march through thick mud in heavy armor, they are furious but fatigued. The mud that has caused them such struggle still bogs them down. This was not how they had been expecting to fight. They are still eager for the fray, but no longer fresh. This is not the easy battle they had been expecting when they woke up this morning.

If it is unpleasant for the French, it is nerve-wracking for the English. Hugely outnumbered, the smallest break in their line will let the French through and overwhelm them. Muscles aching from weeks on the march, famished and weakened, they fight with the strength of desperation.

Part 4:
Enter the Archers

The archers dropped their bows and joined
the defense with swords and axes.
-Michael Lee Lanning

Seeing how bad their situation is, Henry does the only thing he can do to balance the numbers. He unleashes his archers into the brawl.

Abandoning their longbows, the archers draw swords, daggers, and even the heavy mallets they used on their stakes. If failure is a harsh prospect for the men-at-arms, it is an even worse one for these men. The families of captured bowmen cannot not pay ransoms to have them released. If they lose they will be killed by the French, but not killed quickly, they will be tortured first, starting with having their fingers chopped off so they can never again draw a bow string.

Light of foot, the archers dart back and forth through the mud on the French flanks. They stab men-at-arms through gaps in their armor and push others over in the mud. Like fleas on the flanks of a great dog, they buzz at the French column, calling out the English warcry—"St. George!"

Caught up in the mud and chaos of combat, the French advance grinds to a halt. Without the space to maneuver, their numbers start to count against them. They are packed tightly together, unable to move freely, some unable to even lift their weapons to fight. It is hard to parry or dodge the English blows, and all it takes is one slip to end up trampled face down in the mud. Blood lust turns to frustration and anxiety as the chance for honor and glory turns into one for ignominious death. Even retreat is impossible, trapped as they are at the head of the advancing column.

Those behind them have no way of knowing this. Heads and visors still lowered, their view obscured by the press of men, all they have to guide them is the sound of battle and their desire to earn glory and take rich English prisoners. Many of the most famous Frenchmen alive today are in this first wave. They do not know each other well enough to coordinate their efforts, but they are all proud and eager to impress. They push forward over the bodies of their fallen countrymen, only to find themselves bogged down in the same grueling carnage.

The corpses begin to pile up. Men are thrown to the ground by the archers or slip on the treacherous ground. Many drown in the mud or suffocate under the mass of bodies. Others are slaughtered where they lay, pierced or sliced by the daggers of the darting, eager archers.

For the French this is not war, it is hell. At last, those still standing turn and run.

For a moment, the exhausted English can pause for breath. Men-at-arms, soaked with sweat beneath their armor, take a moment to drink water and catch their breath. Nearly all of them are still standing, while around them lay thousands of dead and wounded French. It is a glorious if brutal sight.

To their flanks stand something just as brutal and unnerving, but that they would not give up for all the world. Thousands of archers, mud-spattered and ragged, grinning over the edges of their blood-stained blades.

Part 5:
The Second Wave

Every French man-at-arms worth his salt wanted the honour of striking a blow against the king of England.
-Julet Barker

A brief moment is all the English have. The French second wave is marching towards them through the horror of this muddy field, six thousand men-at-arms and their armed servants led by the Dukes of Bar and Alençon.

The French might look clean and fresh; new knights poured forth from the royal toy box, but they are veterans just like the English, blood-stained in body and soul. Among their ranks are men who had fought on crusade, in wars across Italy, Spain, and Portugal, and in the civil violence that had lately torn France apart.

Their advance is even more difficult than the last, the mud thicker underfoot, their own fleeing countryman blocking their way. Still they come as firm and implacable as the first wave. Up goes the battle-cry from thousands of throats—"Monjoie! St. Denis!" They must drive the enemy from their lands.

Again the English men-at-arms stand ready, the archers hovering eagerly at their flanks. Again the arrows fly and men set themselves to receive the charge. Wearily, they lower their visors and raise their swords once more. With a crash of steel the second French wave hits.

This is a tense moment for the English. They had beaten back one assault, and that raised their spirits, but they are still outnumbered, still bogged down in mud and blood, still exhausted. Men fight with weary determination, and the terrible certainty that there can be no surrender, only triumph or death.

Among the French are a band of eighteen Burgundian squires, young men who had not yet earned the rank of knight. Eager to prove themselves, outraged at what they saw as Henry of

England's insult against their king, they had formed a brotherhood the night before. Together they had sworn an oath to knock the fleur-de-lis, the symbol France, from the front of Henry's crown. They promised to uphold their nation's honor or perish in the attempt.

Through the morass of mud and bodies, these young men come forward. The English are a terrible sight, covered in blood, standing atop mounds of French corpses as they seek a footing from which to fight. The very air is thick with death, the stink of blood and of voided bowels. But these are men of honor, full of the energy of youth. They push through to the front of the line, battering their way through the men facing them. One by one they fall as they advance on Henry's banners. Bloodied and battered, at last they reach him. One of them manages to strike the king, breaking the fleur-de-lis from his ornate helm, before they are all cut down.

They had sworn to do or die. In the end it has been both.

Duke John of Alençon is also eager to reach Henry. Though he had never led a French army to victory, he is a capable fighter with a noble status to maintain. He too fights his way through to the center of the English lines, battering aside those in his way. He fights Humphrey, Duke of Gloucester, King Henry's brother, and strikes him down, injuring him in the leg. Gloucester fell in the mud, at the mercy of Alençon. King Henry, his helm bearing the scar of the earlier attack, leaps to his brother's rescue. The leaders of the French and English forces batter at each other with blades already dented by battle.

Alençon manages to beat the king to his knees. Somehow Henry finds the strength to fight back. Blocking Alençon's blows, he rises once more to his feet. Drawing on whatever energy he still has, he turns the tables on the Duke, beating him into submission. Overwhelmed, Alençon gives in, removing his helmet in a sign of surrender. Alas for Alençon, a knight in Henry's bodyguard, berserk with battle lust and having just seen the danger his king was in, reaches them at this exact moment. Swinging his axe around his head, he smashes it into the Duke's skull, ending his life.

On the brutality rages. All is chaos, men unable to see beyond their own small fragment of the fight. There are no orders, no discipline, just sweat, pain, swinging blades, the screams of the dying, and the crunch of weapons against armor and bone. Henry once more leaps to a comrade's rescue, standing over the wounded Earl of Oxford, fending off the French and saving his life. War might not be a chivalrous adventure, but it is not without courage this day on the part of the young king.

Though the English have taken some losses, the French have suffered many more. Battered in body and spirit, they once more retreat, leaving only the dead and the dying, and those who have surrendered.

Once more Henry's troops can take a moment to catch their breath, and the king has the opportunity to consider his position. Most of his army is still standing, though the Earl of Suffolk lay dead, his closest knights with him. The Duke of York, Henry's fat cousin, is also dead, and a rumor is starting to go around that he suffocated beneath a pile of corpses.

The English marshal their prisoners and tended their wounds, waiting for whatever will come next. Some hope that it is over, but they know that is unlikely.

A cry goes up along the English line—French reinforcements are coming. A third French force is gathering on the far side of the field. The battle is not over.

Before he has time to react, news reaches Henry of an attack in their rear. The baggage camp, a collection of priests and servants guarded by only

a handful of soldiers, is under attack.
   The English are surrounded.

Part 6:
Panic and Slaughter

Sternly the King gave the order, and reluctantly and
hesitantly his soldiers obeyed, for it meant
to them the loss of ransom.
-Alfred H. Burne

Henry believes his army is teetering on the brink of disaster. The enemy are not just to their front and rear—they were among them. If things go badly, those men who have been captured need only to pick up the weapons scattered across the field and the English will find themselves attacked by a force in their very midst.

Henry knows that his men are counting on him

to see them through. Like him, they have faced death that day, and he cannot ask them to needlessly face further danger. He can think now of only one course of action.

So begins what is to become that day's most infamous moment. Henry orders his men to execute all but a handful of prisoners.

Henry's men-at-arms are appalled. Half the reason for coming on this campaign was the chance for profit, and ransoming prisoners is the greatest part of that. More than that, if they show no mercy on nobles like themselves, what could they expect if they in turn are captured? It went against the laws of war. They refuse outright.

So King Henry turns once more to his archers, assigning two hundred of them the task of killing the prisoners. These are men of low standing who will see little or no profit from ransoms, who can expect only mutilation and death if they are captured; men happy to dish out the same swift judgement to keep themselves safe.

What followed is a scene of brutality. Men are cut down where they stand, thinking themselves safe in their captors' mercy. Some are herded into a barn which is quickly set on fire. One of them, Ghillebert de Lannoy, manages to escape the flames. Crawling out on an injured leg, lungs heavy with smoke and the stench of roasting flesh, he escapes the slaughter. The English men-at-arms stand appalled, sickened by the actions of the archers and the order of their king.

Despite the rumors, there is little danger. No reinforcements have come to bolster the French. The third and final line of French troops is made up of rejects, those lacking the skills, the status or the eagerness to be put in the first two assaults. Seeing their fellow countrymen's fate, and witnessing first-hand the brutality of the English, they refuse to attack. The Counts of Marle and Fauquembergues had managed to muster a few hundred mounted men-at-arms, hoping to redeem French honor with a fresh attack, but this pitiful assault fails amid a hail of arrows, never even reaching the English lines.

The attack on the baggage train is no more impressive. A local lord, Isambart d'Agincourt, had gathered six hundred peasants for the attack. This is his contribution to the French battle plan, and it is certainly the most successful part. They are easily chased away, but d'Agincourt's improvised force takes with them English cash, jewels, a royal crown and sword of state, and the official seals of the English chancery. But the damage they have done to their side far outweighs their achievement. The slaughter their attack triggered is never finished, hundreds still live, but many French prisoners died in those moments of panic.

Part 7:
Count the Dead

When the king of England found himself master of the field of battle, and that the French, excepting such as had been killed or taken, were flying in all directions.
-Enguerrand de Monstrelet

After three long hours of carnage, the battle is over. Henry calls over the English and French heralds, who have stood together on the side-lines throughout the fight. As at tournaments, their role was to note the most valiant deeds, to judge who had won and lost, and to keep a record for posterity.

Henry, soaking with sweat, smeared with

blood, muddy and trembling as the energy of battle wares off, faces the senior French herald. Montjoie King of Arms, resplendent in his silken surcoat, stands as representative of his country and arbiter in matters of honor. His appearance could not be more different from that of the king; nor could his mood. Asked by Henry who had won this trial by combat, he reluctantly acknowledges that Henry has won, and that by doing so he has proved the justice of his cause.

In the eyes of God and men, as judged by the laws and culture of the time, Henry is not just the victor—he is right, his cause is just. As sure of his righteousness as Henry had been at the start of the day, he ends it a man whose convictions have led to a brutal conclusion but one amazing victory. He chose the righteousness of his cause and the safety of his army over the rules of honor by which his class is expected to live.

As the day draws to a close, the English count their losses. Many men, including Gloucester, are badly injured, their fates depend on the primitive surgery of the time. But only a small fraction of their force has died, the Duke of York and Earl of Suffolk being the only ones of note. English soldiers scour the field of battle, looting what is worth taking, searching for the injured among their fallen foes. Those who would survive are taken prisoner, but battlefield wounds are hard to treat, and many receive the mercy of a slit throat.

That night, King Henry's high ranking prisoners wait on him at the dinner table. It is a moment for him to gloat, and for them to feel the sting of defeat. But for all that he had won, Henry's image is stained with the blood of noble prisoners. His men-at-arms eye their king and his bowmen warily, relieved to have won, but unsettled by the way that victory has come.

Epilogue

Owre Kynge went forth to Normandy, With grace and myght of chyvalry, Ther God, for hym wrought mervelusly; Wherefore Englonde may call and cry. Deo gratias!
-*Agincourt Carol*

The morning after his decisive victory at the Battle of Agincourt, Henry V ordered his household priests to sing a hymn of thanksgiving for the win. He credited God alone for his victory, the first step in recovering French possessions that he believed belonged to the English crown.

Figures for English losses vary slightly but most widely accepted is around 100 dead. The French suffered heavy losses; about 10,000 troops were killed and 1,500 taken prisoner. The French had been so confident of victory that entire families had gone to battle, and whole family lines came to an end on the battlefield. The captives would present ongoing trouble as Henry refused to accept ransom for them unless they pledged to recognize Henry's claim on the French crown. Many of the prisoners rejected this claim and some remained in English captivity for decades.

The truce between the Armagnac and Burgundian factions quickly evaporate after the loss. Suffering heavy casualties, the Armagnac were blamed for the defeat. Religious decrees tried to explain the defeat with a stress on bad leadership as well as judgment on France for its sins. The Burgundians issued a manifesto charging the Armagnacs with "deliberately permitting Henry V to win the Battle of Agincourt." The Burgundians marched on Paris ten days after the battle to continue the civil war.

Henry quickly returned in triumph to London as a celebrated warrior. He arrived home to London on 23 November 1415 to great public acclaim. He used the victory at the Battle of Agincourt to establish his rights and privileges in France, but the French did not accept this viewpoint. In only two years the French army would force Henry V back onto the battlefield.

Eventually, the Treaty of Troyes, signed in 1420, along with his marriage to Catherine of Valois shortly thereafter, ensured the success of King Henry's campaign to make good on his claim to the French throne. It was a brief success however, he died suddenly in 1422, having been King for less than ten years.

Battle of Agincourt has become one of the most well-known battles of the medieval era, and was one of the most important points in the Hundred Years War between England and France. It is also one of the most powerful examples of the use of the English Longbow in combat. Many books, plays, and songs have been written about the battle, including the Agincourt Carol, written and composed for Henry's return to London after the battle, and Shakespeare's Henry V, written almost 200 years later.

Also note that the traditional date of October 25, 1415 is based on the Julian Calendar. The modern Gregorian Calendar date for this event would have been November 3, 1415.

Bonus:
The English Longbow

England were but a fling, but for the
crooked stick, and the gray goose wing.
-Old English Adage

The English Longbow is an amazing weapon. Also
referred to as the Welsh Longbow, the English
Warbow, the English Great Bow, and sometimes
simply as "the crooked stick," for a period of
several hundred years during the middle ages it
dominated many important battlefields. Used
prominently during the Hundred Years' War (1337-
1453), the English secured wins at Crecy (1346),
Portiers (1356), and as you just read, Agincourt

(1415) with prominent use of the longbow. The English were defeated, however, at Patay (1429) when the archers were caught by the French troops before they could place their typical defensive stakes.

Longbows are a type of "self bow," which means they are constructed from a single, solid piece of wood and were sized to fit their user; most were around six feed in length from top to bottom. The best longbows were made from yew wood, but they could also be constructed from boxwood, ash, or elm. It took several hours for a master bowyer to carve the valuable yew staves into the proper shape for a longbow and several years of drying until they were ready to be used in combat.

Archery practice was essentially a compulsory activity for English peasants during certain times of the middle ages, sometimes even being the only sport or game that was allowed on Sundays. This was because learning to use the English Warbow was not an easy task, it took years and training that started during childhood; having archery as the national sport ensured the military would have plenty of archers ready for battle.

With a considerable amount of force required to cause the swift and forceful flight of the arrow, it took at least 80 pounds of pull and perhaps even as much as 200 pounds of force to pull the bow string all the way back. A typical English archer could release up to 12 arrows per minute at full draw length to rain down metal points on enemies up to 200 yards away.

Besides the simple target arrows used for practice, two main types of arrowheads were typically used in battle, a bodkin for armored targets and a broadhead for unarmored. Bodkins had long, thin points and were designed specifically for piercing either chain-mail or plate armor. Broadheads came in a variety of styles but included sharp edges that were designed to tear gashes in the flesh of men and horses to cause bleeding.

Since they were made from simple pieces of wood that deteriorated over time, only a few hundred examples of medieval longbows still exist today.

Most of those remaining longbows are from the Mary Rose, an English ship that was constructed less than 100 years after the Battle of Agincourt, under the reign of Henry VIII, and which subsequently sank in the English channel 33 years later during a French attack. The Mary Rose was salvaged in 1982 and contained many important historical artifacts, including over 200 well-preserved English Longbows which have been carefully studied and used for numerous scientific tests and replica projects.

Today, many groups and individuals around the world are dedicated to preserving traditional archery and English-style longbows can easily be purchased online or in archery shops for target shooting or even hunting.

Online Resources

The text of this book is just the first step in what we provide to help you learn about the Battle of Agincourt. The online resources include recommended additional reading, a complete bibliography for this work, links to interesting videos, and more.

Plus you can download a free draft copy of our next DecisiveDays book!

For the online resources, please visit:
DecisiveDays.com/agincourt

About the Author/Publisher

DecisiveDays produces a series of short narratives on important days in history.

We have upcoming books planned on the battles of Waterloo, Sterling Bridge, Zama, and more. Check out our website and social media pages to keep up-to-date.

DecisiveDays.com

facebook.com/DecisiveDays

twitter.com/DecisiveDays

Feedback

Reviews on Amazon.com are the best way to give us feedback. Type the below address into your browser to be directed straight to Amazon's review page for this book. Then, simply click on the "Create your own review" button.

decisivedays.com/rev1

You can also email us at any time with questions, comments, feedback, or suggestions.

news@decisivedays.com

www.ingramcontent.com/pod-product-compliance
Lightning Source LLC
Chambersburg PA
CBHW060624030426

42337CB00018B/3180